Butterflies,
Skippers, and Moths

By James S. Ayars
and
Milton W. Sanderson

Illustrated by
Carl and Mary Hauge

WHITMAN PUBLISHING COMPANY
RACINE, WISCONSIN

contents

Library of Congress Catalog Card Number: 64-10931

Copyright © 1964 by Whitman Publishing Company
Printed in the U.S.A. by Western Printing and Lithographing Company
All Rights Reserved

Flying Flowers?

A BUTTERFLY, flitting and gliding across a sunlit pasture, settles suddenly on a tall plant. A moth at dusk hovers over a bed of petunias.

What does the tall plant mean to the butterfly? What do the petunias mean to the moth?

For countless centuries men have asked such questions. They have admired the beauty of butterflies and their relatives and wondered about their strange ways.

Some butterflies have such brilliant colors that poetic people have called them flying flowers. Some fly so airily that the ancient Greeks thought of them as symbols of Zephyros, god of the gentle west wind.

Butterflies may serve very well as symbols of an ancient Greek god. But they are not flowers. They are insects. So are their close relatives, the skippers and the moths.

The Lepidoptera

IN MANY WAYS, butterflies, skippers, and moths are like other insects. They have six legs. Their bodies have three main parts: a head, a thorax or "chest," and an abdomen.

Like many other insects, they have four stages: egg, larva, pupa, and adult. The larva of a butterfly, skipper, or moth is often called a caterpillar. In many moths the pupa has a silken outer covering called a cocoon. The pupa of a butterfly is usually called a chrysalis. It has no outer covering like the cocoon of a moth.

The caterpillar hatches from the egg. It spends its time moving about, eating, and growing. Its outside covering or skin does not stretch. So, as the caterpillar grows, it has to molt, or shed its skin, several times—usually five times. The periods between molts are known as *instars*.

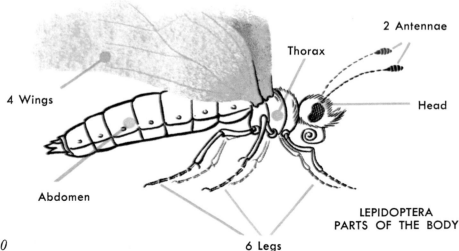

2 Antennae

Thorax

4 Wings

Head

Abdomen

LEPIDOPTERA
PARTS OF THE BODY

10

6 Legs

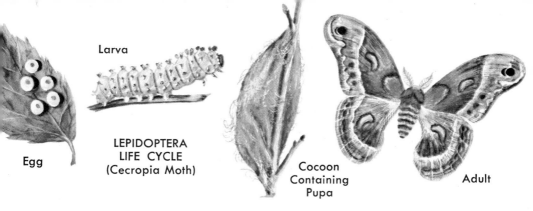

Egg

Larva

**LEPIDOPTERA
LIFE CYCLE
(Cecropia Moth)**

Cocoon
Containing
Pupa

Adult

At the end of the last instar, the caterpillar stops eating and prepares to become a pupa or chrysalis. The pupa appears to be lifeless, or at least sleeping. But great changes take place within the pupal case. After a while, sometimes months later, a winged insect emerges, comes out of the case. This is an adult. Male and female adults mate, and the females lay the eggs from which caterpillars hatch.

In one way, at least, butterflies, skippers, and moths are different from other insects. They are the *Lepidoptera,* the flaky-winged or scaly-winged insects. The tiny hairs on their wings are flattened to form flakes or scales, each so small that it can hardly be seen with the naked eye.

The scientific name for these insects comes from two Greek words. *Lepid* means flakelike or scalelike; *ptera* means feather or wing.

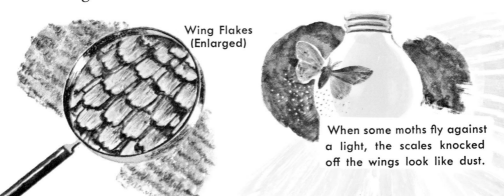

Wing Flakes
(Enlarged)

When some moths fly against
a light, the scales knocked
off the wings look like dust.

Which Is It?

A BUTTERFLY, a skipper, or a moth—which is it?

If it does its flying in the daytime, it is probably a butterfly or a skipper. If it has bright-colored wings, it is probably a butterfly. But some moths fly in the daytime, and some moths and skippers have bright-colored wings.

In some ways, a few moths are like most butterflies, and a few butterflies are like most moths. Skippers are the in-between Lepidoptera. They are in some ways like typical moths, but in more ways like typical butterflies.

The outline on these pages will help you to tell butterflies from moths, and skippers from both moths and butterflies.

12

BUTTERFLY

Monarch Butterfly

SKIPPER

Silver Spotted Skipper
(Underside View
Showing Spots)

MOTH

Cecropia Moth

Active during
daylight hours.

Usually rest
with wings
folded togeth-
er over back.

With bright-
colored wings
(most of them).

Antennae are
swollen at
ends, not re-
curved or
hooked.

Active during
daylight hours.

Usually rest
with wings
held at an an-
gle over back.

With dull-col-
ored wings
(many of them).

Antennae are
swollen at ends
and recurved
or hooked.

Active only at
night (most of
them).

Usually rest
with wings
spread and
held flat.

With dull-col-
ored wings
(many of them).

Antennae are
of various
forms, in most
kinds not swol-
len at tip.

A Common Butterfly

ONE OF the commonest species, or kinds, of butterflies is the monarch. Yet it lives a life so full of danger that it ought to be rare. Its larva feeds on only one type of plant. It passes the winter in the delicate adult stage. And it migrates long distances.

In February, monarch butterflies start northward from the southern United States and Central America, where they have spent the winter. They fly during the day and at night roost in trees. They stop their flights only briefly to suck nectar from chinaberry, spirea, lilac, milkweed, and other common blossoms.

On the undersides of the leaves of young milkweed plants, each female lays her cream-colored eggs—singly, but as many as four hundred in all. Only milkweed plants—fourteen or more species—will do as food for the young larvae or caterpillars that will hatch from the eggs in three to five days.

As a caterpillar emerges from the egg, it is about one-twelfth of an inch long. It has a grayish-white body and a shiny black head. It eats some of the eggshell and then starts feeding on a leaf.

When its body has grown too large for its skin, the caterpillar is ready to molt. It spins a silken web. Then, clinging

A human being who grew as much as a monarch caterpillar would be thirty-five to forty feet tall.

to the web with its legs, it wriggles its body until the old skin splits. Then it crawls out. The molt may take several hours.

The caterpillar continues to feed, grow, and molt. With each molt, its body is larger. In the fifth stage or instar, the caterpillar is a cream color or yellow with dark brown or black bands. It can be easily seen on a milkweed leaf. If the leaf is touched the caterpillar may drop off the leaf and "play 'possum."

The caterpillar has an enormous appetite. It may eat a leaf in four minutes and rest for only fifteen minutes before it begins eating again. In ten to twenty-eight days, it is ready to pupate. Then it may weigh hundreds of times as much as when it was hatched.

Late in the fifth instar the caterpillar becomes restless. It leaves its food plant and explores for a place to pupate under a log or leaf or on a tree limb. There it spins two layers of

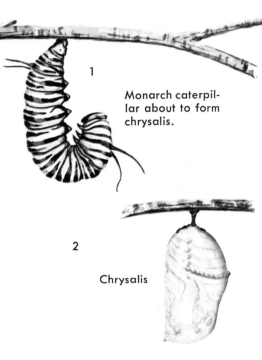

1

Monarch caterpillar about to form chrysalis.

2

Chrysalis

silk with its mouth. Then, grasping the silk with the tip of its abdomen, it hangs head down, its body forming a U or J. The yellow of its body becomes a blue-green. The front end of its body swells and its skin breaks. In about a day, the pupa frees itself from its larval skin. Now hanging from silken threads is a beautiful chrysalis, robin's egg blue dotted with gold.

In nine to fifteen days, an insect with wings develops inside the chrysalis. The skin splits and the winged insect, a butterfly, pushes out a pair of legs and grasps the outside of the chrysalis. It needs only about four minutes to work its head and body out of the chrysalis. Its wings are so limp and crumpled that the butterfly cannot fly.

16

3

Adult monarch butterfly emerging from chrysalis.

As it hangs suspended from the chrysalis, it slowly moves its wings up and down, and fluid from the body is pumped into the wings. Gradually the wings grow larger. In ten to twenty minutes, they are full size.

Monarchs emerging in spring and early summer migrate northward. On the way, they mate, and the females lay eggs. Young hatch. As cold weather approaches, the new monarchs start southward. Sometimes they gather in great numbers just before and during the southward migration.

Of the many millions of monarchs that start the southward migration, only a few reach the wintering grounds. Rough weather is their worst enemy.

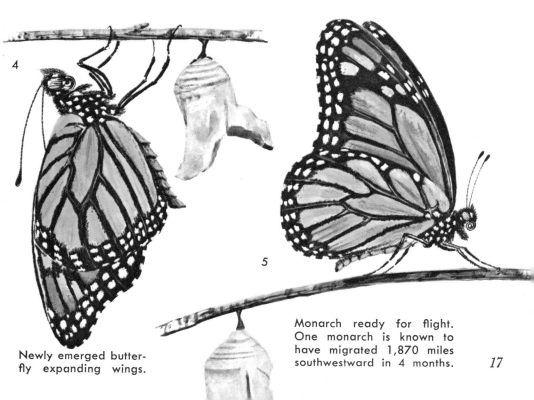

4

5

Newly emerged butterfly expanding wings.

Monarch ready for flight. One monarch is known to have migrated 1,870 miles southwestward in 4 months.

17

Other Common Butterflies

SOME KINDS of butterflies are common in all or most parts of North America. Some are common in only a few places. Some are rare.

Each kind of butterfly depends on certain kinds of plants as food for the adults or their caterpillars. Each kind usually is found on or near the plants that either the adults or the caterpillars feed on.

The females of each kind of butterfly lay their eggs on only certain kinds of plants. In some mysterious way, the females seem to sense which kinds of plants will serve as food for the caterpillars that hatch from their eggs.

The kinds of butterflies common in many places are those that depend on plants that are also common in many places.

Some of the common and widely distributed butterflies are pictured on this and the following five pages.

VICEROY
The viceroy is a butterfly of meadows and roadsides. It looks so much like the monarch that it is sometimes called the mimic. It is found all over the United States except the Northwest. The viceroy larva feeds on the leaves of several common plants, including willow, poplar, oak, and apple trees.

RED-SPOTTED PURPLE
Between the Atlantic Ocean and the Rocky Mountains the red-spotted purple is nearly as common as its relative the viceroy. The undersides of its wings have many red marks often not found on the upper sides. This butterfly overwinters as a part-grown larva. The larva feeds on many plants of the rose, plum, apple, and willow families.

RED ADMIRAL
The red admiral, a butterfly of North America, Europe, Asia, and Africa, overwinters either as an adult or a pupa. The food of the larva is chiefly nettles. The adult, which flies very rapidly, often zigzagging, is seen mostly in woods and along woodland roads.

PAINTED LADY
The painted lady, or thistle butterfly, is found in nearly every part of the world where thistles and related plants are present for the larva to eat. It is believed to be the most widely distributed of all butterflies. Often the adults migrate, possibly because of a shortage of food for the larvae. This butterfly has a rapid flight like that of the red admiral, but it spends more time in feeding on flowers.

GREAT SPANGLED FRITILLARY

The great spangled fritillary, noted for its large size and arrangement of silver spots on the undersides of the hind wings, is found in most of Canada and the United States. It can be seen during the day, flying rapidly over open fields, visiting the flowers of milkweeds, thistles, and many other plants. The larva feeds only on violets and only at night; it hides close to the ground during the day.

WOOD NYMPH

The wood nymph, also known as the grayling, is usually seen flying close to the ground in woodlands or perched on tree trunks. It is found in much of Canada and the United States and parts of Mexico. The larva feeds only on grasses. The adults vary in color and size.

PEARL CRESCENT

A small butterfly that is seen darting after another butterfly too near its perch may be the pearl crescent. It may be seen in meadows and along roadsides in most of North America. Asters are the chief food plants of the larva.

BLACK SWALLOWTAIL

Often called the parsnip swallowtail, the black swallowtail is found in open spaces throughout North America. Unlike many other butterflies, it sometimes rests on flowers with its wings only half closed. The larva feeds on parsnip and such closely related plants as carrot, parsley, and dill. Sometimes it is so abundant that it becomes a pest.

PIPE-VINE SWALLOWTAIL

The pipe-vine swallowtail, found in many parts of the United States, is sometimes called the blue swallowtail. The adult sucks the nectar of many kinds of woodland flowers, including orchids. The larva feeds on Dutchman's pipe—its favorite food—wild ginger, and knotweeds. This swallowtail passes the winter as either an adult or a pupa.

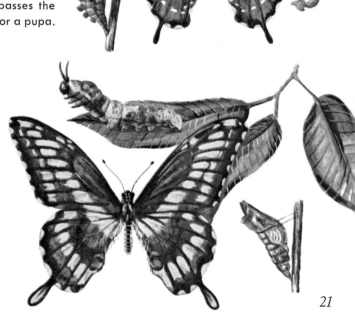

GIANT SWALLOWTAIL

The giant swallowtail is the largest butterfly and one of the most colorful in the United States. It may be found flying in or near woodlands or orchards. Its larva, called the "orange dog," feeds on the leaves of orange and other citrus trees, or, where these trees do not grow, it feeds on prickly ash, hop tree, or wafer ash.

21

ALFALFA BUTTERFLY

The alfalfa butterfly, or orange sulphur, is found almost everywhere in North America from southern Canada to Mexico. The larva feeds on alfalfa and other plants in the pea family. An alfalfa field with thousands of orange sulphurs dancing over it is a beautiful sight.

CHECKERED WHITE

The checkered white lives in most of North America. It is a native of this continent. The larva, like the larva of its relative, the European cabbage butterfly, eats cabbage, mustard, and related plants, but it is less common and does less damage.

CLOUDED SULPHUR

The clouded sulphur, sometimes called the mud puddle butterfly, lives in all North America from Alaska to the southern United States. Its larva eats about the same plants as the larva of the alfalfa butterfly. These two butterflies are so closely related that sometimes they cross or hybridize.

SPRING AZURE
One of the earliest of butterflies each year is the spring azure. Its first appearance about mud puddles in spring was once the signal for Oklahoma boys to go barefoot. This small butterfly is found throughout the United States and Canada. The larva feeds on the flower buds of many kinds of plants.

AMERICAN COPPER
The American copper, one of the daintiest of butterflies, is one of the worst tempered. It may "buzz" larger butterflies or anything else that moves. It is commonly seen in open fields, where the larva finds its only known food plants, sheep sorrels and docks. This butterfly lives in many parts of the United States and Canada.

SNOUT BUTTERFLY
The snout butterfly is easy to recognize by its small size and long, beaklike mouth. It likes roadsides and muddy stream margins near woodlands, and open fields where it finds hackberry and wolfberry, favorite foods of the larva. It is found in most parts of the United States except the Northwest.

Not So Common Butterflies

CLIMATE, as well as food, is very important to butterflies. Each kind of butterfly must have certain kinds of climate, just as it must have certain kinds of food. A particular kind of butterfly cannot live in a part of the country where the climate is too cold for it, or too hot or too dry or too wet or too windy, even if its food plants are there.

For one reason or another, the butterflies pictured on this and the following page are not found in as many parts of North America as the kinds shown on pages 18 to 23.

WHITE ADMIRAL
A butterfly of the open forest and forest edges, the white admiral is found in the northeastern United States and adjoining Canada as far west as the Great Lakes. In feeding, it visits flowers and sometimes dead animals and excrement. Large numbers may gather about wet spots. Its larva feeds chiefly on birch, willow, poplar, and hawthorn.

LITTLE WOOD SATYR
The little wood satyr lives in woodlands and in shaded grassy areas nearby. It flies close to the ground, expertly weaving its way through tall grass. Often it flies during cloudy weather, even in rain. It is found only in the eastern United States and southeastern Canada. Its larva feeds on grasses.

ZEBRA SWALLOWTAIL

The beautiful zebra swallowtail is found only in the eastern half of the United States and in a small part of Canada in which the pawpaw, the food plant of the larva, grows. This butterfly varies with the season in size or color or in length of tail.

PARNASSIUS BUTTERFLY

Parnassius phoebus belongs to a small group sometimes called the apollo butterflies. This species, a tailless relative of the swallowtails, usually lives on high mountains. It is found from Alaska to California and New Mexico, and also in parts of Europe and Asia. The larva feeds on stonecrop and saxifrage, usually growing on rocks or stony ground.

ZEBRA BUTTERFLY OR LONG WING

In the United States, the zebra butterfly, or long wing, lives only near the Gulf Coast. However, it lives also in the West Indies, South America, and Central America. It is distasteful to birds. Zebras gather in colonies to sleep at night, but scatter to feed during daytime. The larva feeds on the passion-flower.

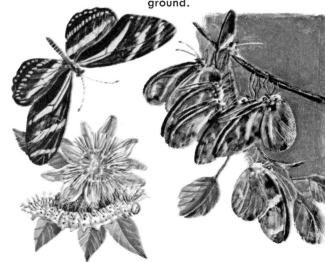

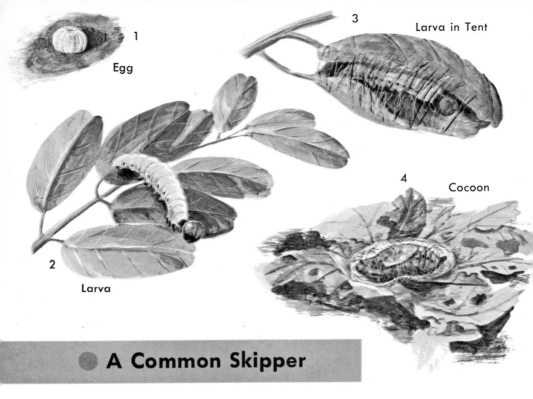

1 Egg

3 Larva in Tent

4 Cocoon

2 Larva

● A Common Skipper

NEARLY two hundred different kinds of skippers have been found in North America, but few of them are known to the average butterfly collector. They are hard to catch, and some are hard to identify or tell apart.

One of the best known and handsomest is the silver-spotted skipper, which is common in most of the area from southern Canada to South America.

This skipper passes the winter as a pupa. The adult emerges in spring. After mating, the female lays her tiny eggs on the upper surface of a leaf, usually the leaf of a locust tree.

In about a week a larva with a yellow body, a narrow neck,

Skipper in Flight
(Underside)

5

Silver Spotted Skipper
Adult

and a brownish-red head hatches from an egg.

The larva or caterpillar encloses itself in a tiny tent that it makes from a leaf and silk threads from its body. The caterpillar soon molts, outgrows its first tent, and makes another tent of two leaves held together by silk threads. During the day, the caterpillar is not active, but at night it crawls out of its tent to feed upon leaves of the plant on which it is living.

After its final molt, the caterpillar leaves its tent and crawls to the ground. There, among fallen leaves, it spins a cocoon in which it lives quietly through the winter.

When the warm weather of spring arrives, the cocoon is split and an insect with damp, bedraggled wings emerges. In a short time the wings are dry and the skipper has started its darting flight.

In the northern part of its range, the silver-spotted skipper has one brood each year. Farther south, it has two or three broods a year.

27

Cecropia Moth

● A Common Moth

THE HANDSOME cecropia, with a wingspread of five to six inches, is one of the few North American silkworm moths. It is common in the United States from the Atlantic Coast westward to the Great Plains. Two close relatives that look like it but are smaller live in the western states. They are Glover's silk moth and the Ceanothus silk moth.

The cecropia lives through the winter as a pupa in a silken case or cocoon. The case, usually grayish or brown and about three inches long, is attached to a twig or branch of one of more than fifty food plants, which include the maple, willow, lilac, elm, apple, hawthorn, cottonwood, and box elder.

In spring the cecropia finishes changing from a caterpillar to a winged insect, splits the pupal case, and emerges through the end of the cocoon. Six to eight hours later, the wings are dry and full size.

Within twenty-four to forty-eight hours, adults mate. The female lays two hundred to three hundred chalky white eggs, each less than one-eighth inch long.

In twelve to fourteen days, a caterpillar is ready to hatch

28

from each egg. It starts chipping away at the shell on the inside. Twenty to forty-five minutes later, it has made an opening and crawled out.

The caterpillar starts feeding at once, first on the shell of the egg and then on the nearest leaf. After a few days of ravenous feeding, it has a body too large for its skin. So it molts. It spins a floor of silk on which to stand as it draws its body out of the end of the skin.

For several weeks the cecropia caterpillar keeps on eating, growing, and molting. By late summer or early fall it is in the fifth stage or instar. It spins a silken cocoon attached to a twig of the plant it has been feeding on. Then it is ready for winter.

Cecropia cocoons are favorites with collectors. Good places to look for them are on willows along streams or on apple trees in orchards. The cocoons should be kept outdoors until January or February. Then they may be brought inside the house, where high temperatures will force the moths to emerge early.

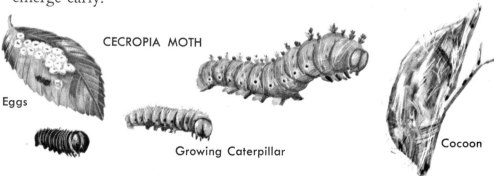

CECROPIA MOTH

Eggs

Growing Caterpillar

Cocoon

As the caterpillar emerges from the egg, it is black and about a quarter inch long. Its head is as wide as its body. After a few days of hearty eating, it outgrows its skin and molts. Emerging from the old skin, it is dusky green and about a half inch long. Its head is about half as wide as its body. The caterpillar grows and molts several times until it spins its cocoon.

● Other Moths

To MOTHS, as well as butterflies, food and climate are very important. No kind of moth can live for very long except where it finds food and climate suitable for its larvae and adults. Some of the moths on this and the following two pages are common. Some are rare.

LUNA MOTH

From May to August, the pale green luna moth is on the wing. It is a favorite with amateur collectors. The larva, at first green and later dark brown, feeds on the leaves of walnut, hickory, persimmon, and many other trees. This insect passes the winter on the ground as a cocoon in a single tough, thin layer of brown silk. It is fairly common in the United States east of the Great Plains.

IO MOTH

The io moth rests with its wings folded to form a triangle. The male is smaller and lighter in color than the female. The larva feeds on the leaves of cotton plants and many kinds of trees and shrubs. When young, the larvae move in single file and line up abreast when feeding. This moth is found from the Atlantic Coast to Colorado and New Mexico.

REGAL MOTH

From an egg of the beautiful regal moth hatches a larva that is as frightening as its name, the hickory horned devil. This, the largest of North American caterpillars, feeds on leaves of hickory, butternut, black walnut, and several other trees. The regal moth is found in most of the eastern United States.

BROWN DAY MOTH

Unlike most moths, the brown day moth is active when the sun is shining brightly. It is found from Colorado to the Pacific Coast. When fall comes the female lays eggs that hatch the following spring. The larva feeds on many kinds of plants, including willow, manzanita, blackberry, and wild rose.

ISABELLA TIGER MOTH

The Isabella tiger moth is found throughout the United States. Better known than the adult is the caterpiller, called the banded woolly bear. The New England saying, "hurrying along like a caterpillar in the fall," gives a good picture of the woolly bear. In autumn this caterpillar may be seen scurrying across a highway to find shelter in or near the ground before winter begins. In spring it makes a cocoon, mostly of hair. The adult emerges in May.

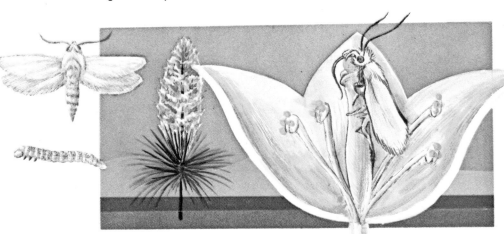

YUCCA MOTH

Flowers of the yucca plant are open only one night each year. The female yucca moth emerges from her pupa at the same time and mates with a male. She scrapes the pollen from a yucca flower and flies with it to another yucca flower. There she lays her eggs in one part of the flower and leaves the pollen in another part to make sure that the flower will be fertilized and have seeds for her young when they hatch. Without the plant, the moth could not survive. Without the moth, the plant could not survive.

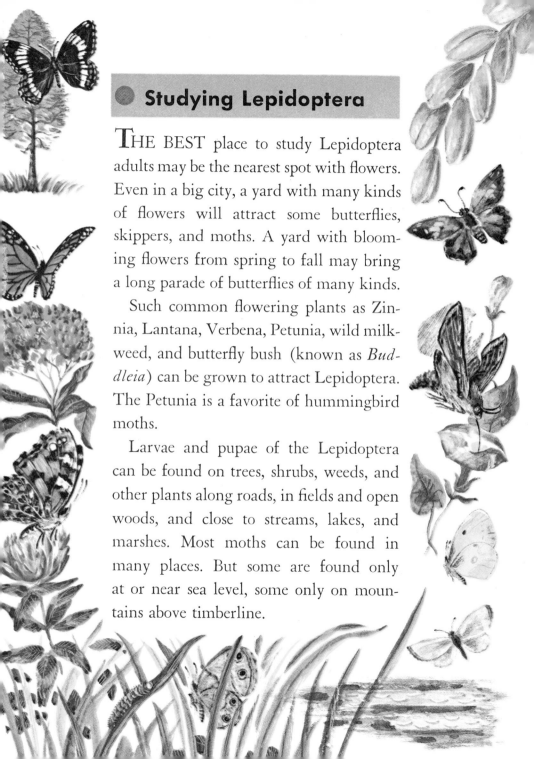

Studying Lepidoptera

THE BEST place to study Lepidoptera adults may be the nearest spot with flowers. Even in a big city, a yard with many kinds of flowers will attract some butterflies, skippers, and moths. A yard with blooming flowers from spring to fall may bring a long parade of butterflies of many kinds.

Such common flowering plants as Zinnia, Lantana, Verbena, Petunia, wild milkweed, and butterfly bush (known as *Buddleia*) can be grown to attract Lepidoptera. The Petunia is a favorite of hummingbird moths.

Larvae and pupae of the Lepidoptera can be found on trees, shrubs, weeds, and other plants along roads, in fields and open woods, and close to streams, lakes, and marshes. Most moths can be found in many places. But some are found only at or near sea level, some only on mountains above timberline.

Collectors and Books

MUCH CAN BE LEARNED about butterflies and moths simply by watching them. More can be learned about them by reading books—books that tell how the Lepidoptera live, books with many pictures that help identify the different kinds or species. No one book is big enough to include all Lepidoptera.

Still more can be learned about butterflies and moths by collecting them and by talking to other collectors.

Many museums, colleges, and universities have Lepidoptera collections. Some have professional Lepidopterists—people who are paid for studying butterflies, skippers, and moths.

Expert Lepidopterists willing to help beginners may point out better ways of collecting specimens and identifying them. They may show ways in which collections can be made of great value to science, or offer to trade specimens.

Life Histories

Egg

MOST LEPIDOPTERA pass through the stages described for the monarch butterfly. This series of stages is called the life history.

There are slight differences among the life histories. Some Lepidoptera take much longer than others to pass through the different stages. Most Lepidoptera larvae molt five or six times, but a few occasionally molt more times. Most Lepidoptera adults have wings, but in a few species of moths the females are without wings. Some kinds of Lepidoptera have only one generation (life cycle) a year. Some have two or more generations. Some Lepidoptera live through the winter as pupae, some as larvae, and a few as adults.

Life histories of Lepidoptera are like biographies of people.

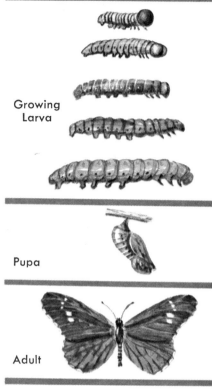

Growing Larva

Pupa

Adult

Egg

The small larva hatches from an egg. As it eats and grows, the larva becomes too large for its skin; so it molts, shedding its old outgrown skin for a new one.

After the last instar, the larva becomes a pupa. The pupa after many internal changes becomes an adult. The adults mate, and the female lays eggs. From each of these eggs a new larva may hatch.

How Lepidoptera Eat

THE ADULTS and the larvae of the Lepidoptera are not at all alike in the food they eat and in the way they eat it. The adults of most kinds suck only the nectar or juices of flowers. The larvae tear off, chew, and swallow the leaves and other parts of plants.

Each adult of most kinds of Lepidoptera has a tongue or proboscis like a tiny soda straw, which it uses as a sucking tube. This it usually keeps coiled like a watch spring. When an adult alights on a flower, the tongue uncoils and is thrust deep into the flower to reach the little wells of nectar. At the back of the tongue is a pumplike structure that helps the adult to suck in the nectar. The ancient ancestors of butterflies and

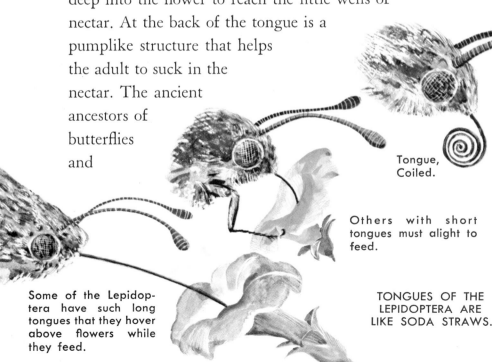

Tongue, Coiled.

Others with short tongues must alight to feed.

Some of the Lepidoptera have such long tongues that they hover above flowers while they feed.

TONGUES OF THE LEPIDOPTERA ARE LIKE SODA STRAWS.

moths had jaws, but in most Lepidoptera adults living today only useless nubs appear where jaws might be.

Not all Lepidoptera adults feed on nectar in the usual way described. Some eat nothing throughout adult life. The cotton leaf moth and some others feed on fruit juices. They have beaks with sharp spines that can puncture the skin of fruit.

The Lepidoptera larva or caterpillar has a pair of large jaws or mandibles for tearing off and chewing food. Some kinds of larvae eat only leaves, stems, or roots. Other kinds eat flowers, fruit, or seeds. Still others live and feed only inside stems or branches of plants. Some of those that eat leaves are called miners. They live inside the leaves and eat only the middle layer between the upper and lower surfaces. Unlike the thick mandibles of most other larvae the mandibles of leaf-mining larvae are flattened like knife blades.

Spined beak, cotton leaf moth.

Jaws of average larva.

Larva shown here between two surfaces of a leaf.

MOUTH PARTS OF THE LEPIDOPTERA ARE ADAPTED TO THE KINDS OF FOOD THEY EAT.

Flattened jaws, leaf mining larva.

● How to Start a Collection

ANYONE who makes a serious study of butterflies, skippers, or moths will soon want to examine them closely. Examining them closely will mean collecting them. And collecting them may mean starting an exciting hobby.

Making a butterfly or moth collection includes more than collecting butterflies or moths. It includes catching and killing them without unnecessary damage, mounting them on pins, identifying and labeling them, and storing them neatly where they will be safe from insect-eating insects and careless human beings.

The first piece of equipment needed for making a collection of butterflies, skippers, or moths is a net. Other items needed are one or more killing jars, spreading boards, relaxers, and storage boxes. Special kinds of long, slender pins called insect pins also are needed.

For about two dollars, a net can be purchased—usually in a sporting goods or toy store. Or a net can be made from a wire loop twelve to fifteen inches in diameter, a bag about two feet long of some fine material like marquisette or nylon netting, and a handle thirty-six to forty inches long.

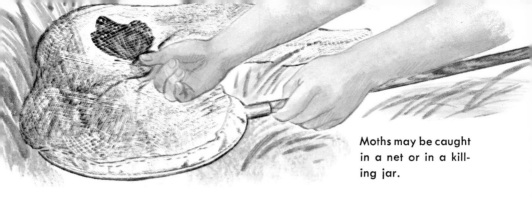

Moths may be caught in a net or in a killing jar.

In using a net for catching a butterfly or skipper, swing the net down on the insect from above. Corner the insect in the net; grasp it by the thorax and give a gentle squeeze to keep it from beating its wings against the net.

A jar for killing the insects can be made from a mayonnaise or pickle jar wide enough to hold a large butterfly. Place a tightly crumpled piece of tissue paper in the jar and pour several drops of amyl acetate (fingernail polish thinner) on the paper. Cover the crumpled paper with more crumpled paper so the amyl acetate cannot touch any insect placed in the jar. Keep the jar covered with a tight-fitting lid except when putting in or taking out insects.

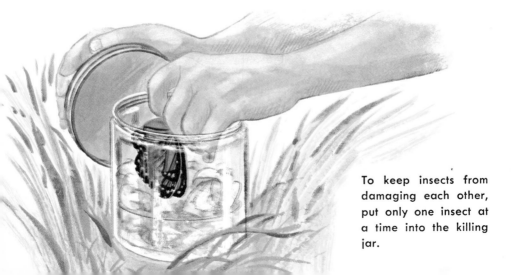

To keep insects from damaging each other, put only one insect at a time into the killing jar.

The spreading board, used for keeping the wings of butter-flies, skippers, and moths in the proper shape while the insects are drying, can be bought from a scientific supply company. You can also make one as shown in the drawing.

The relaxer, used for softening insects that have hardened before they could be mounted, can be made from a wide-mouth jar with a screw-on lid. Place about an inch of clean sand in the bottom of the jar. Wet the sand well with water, and place an overturned jar lid on the sand. Put only a few insects on the jar lid at any one time and cover the jar tightly. In a day or two the insects will be soft and pliable enough to be placed on the spreading board.

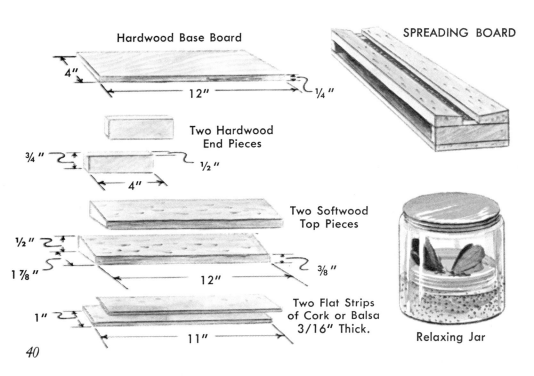

Hardwood Base Board

SPREADING BOARD

4"

12"

1/4"

Two Hardwood End Pieces

3/4"

1/2"

4"

Two Softwood Top Pieces

1/2"

1 7/8"

12"

3/8"

1"

11"

Two Flat Strips of Cork or Balsa 3/16" Thick.

Relaxing Jar

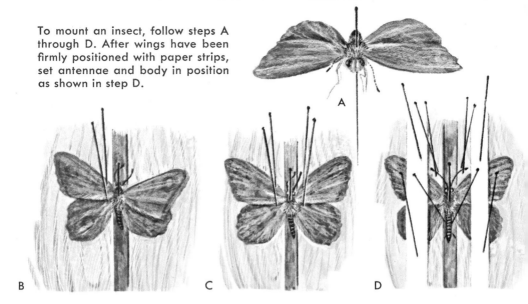

To mount an insect, follow steps A through D. After wings have been firmly positioned with paper strips, set antennae and body in position as shown in step D.

A

B

C

D

Select an insect pin of the right size for the specimen to be mounted. Run the pin through the thorax between the wings of the insect until only about half an inch of the pin can be seen above it. Then push the point of the pin gently into the balsa or cork in the groove of the spreading board. Let the wings of the insect rest on the sloping sides of the spreading board. Place a pin behind the hard front edge of the front wing and move this wing forward until the back edge of the wing is straight out from the body. Move the back wing forward until the insect looks most attractive. Then hold the wings flat with broad strips of paper. When all wings have been put in place, set the insect on the board in a safe place to dry. In about two weeks it will be dry enough to be removed from the board for labeling and storing.

41

Special Collecting Methods

BUTTERFLIES and skippers, active in daylight, are easily seen, even though sometimes hard to net. Most of the moths, usually active only at night, are harder to see and special collecting methods may be needed.

Many moths are attracted to lights and may be collected at brightly lighted store windows or automobile service stations.

"Sugaring" has long been a favorite method of collecting moths. A mixture of sugar, molasses, yeast, water, and perhaps decaying fruit is allowed to sit and ferment for a few days. Then the mixture is painted on tree trunks or fence

posts near woodlands or other places where moths are likely to be. A flashlight trained on the painted spots at night will probably reveal some moths that do not come to lights.

An especially interesting way of collecting Lepidoptera is by rearing them from eggs or larvae.

42

Place larvae in a box with leaves from the plant from which the larvae were collected. Keep the box in a shady spot, such as a screened porch. Supply fresh leaves as often as necessary, which may be very often, as hungry larvae eat almost constantly. Place a layer of soil in the bottom of the box, as some larvae pupate in soil.

If you have collected eggs instead of larvae, watch for the eggs to hatch. Then supply leaves from the kind of plant on which the eggs were laid.

Keep a record of when the eggs hatch, when the larvae pupate, and when each butterfly, skipper, or moth emerges from its crysalis or cocoon.

Try raising Lepidoptera for your collection. Gather eggs or larvae and place them in dirt-filled boxes with the kinds of food each needs. In time, you can watch as the adults emerge.

Identifying Specimens

THE SIMPLEST way for a beginning collector to find the name of a butterfly, skipper, or moth is to turn the pages of a good Lepidoptera book until he finds a picture that matches the specimen.

Some kinds of Lepidoptera are easy to name or identify. They look like no other kinds. Among these are the luna moth and the zebra swallowtail butterfly.

Some kinds are so much like other kinds in size, shape, color, or pattern that at first the beginning collector can see no difference. For example, he may have two specimens that he believes are painted beauties. Actually, he may have a painted beauty and a painted lady. A look at the underside of the hind wings will show two large eye spots on one speci-

The male of the alfalfa butterfly has a solid dark border on the outer margin of each wing; the female has light yellow spots on the dark border.

(Male)

Alfalfa Butterfly

(Female)

Alfalfa Butterfly

Monarch

Viceroy

Some of the Lepidoptera seem to mimic others. The viceroy looks and acts like the monarch. But the viceroy is smaller, and across each hind wing is a narrow dark mark the monarch does not have.

men (this is the painted beauty) and three to five smaller spots on the other (this is the painted lady).

Identifying Lepidoptera specimens is like detective work. It takes time, patience, and attention to details. Clues sometimes come from unexpected places—like the undersides of wings.

In some kinds of Lepidoptera, the male and female differ in color or size. The female of the imperial moth is much larger and is lighter in color than the male.

Among the most familiar North American butterflies are the tiger swallowtails. Four species look so much alike they are hard to tell apart. One species lives mostly east of the Rocky Mountains, three species mostly west. Yet two, three, or four species can be found in some localities. To complicate matters more, the eastern species has a dark form—some females so dark they can easily be mistaken for black species.

● Labeling Specimens

ON THE PIN of every butterfly, skipper, or moth that goes into a collection should be one or more small labels. On one label should be the name of the place where the specimen was captured, the date of capture, and the name of the collector. For example, if Jack Miller caught a painted lady butterfly in Chicago, Illinois, on August 27, 1963, this information would be printed with black India ink and a crow quill pen on a small rectangle cut from a 3 by 5 card.

Also on the pin may be two other labels. One may have on it the name of the flower from which the butterfly was collected and the other the name of the specimen.

All information of this kind is important to scientists who study the Lepidoptera. These scientists need to know where certain species live, when they are active, and what plants they feed on.

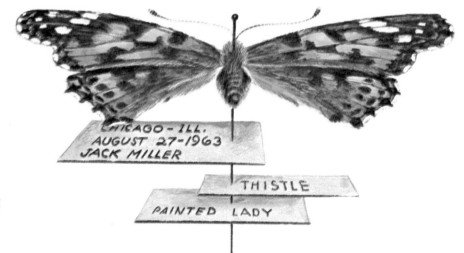

Many Lepidoptera have two kinds of names—common and scientific. Some have several common names. A butterfly may have a different common name for each country or region it lives in. The scientific name of a butterfly or any other insect is supposed to be the same in all parts of the world. *Vanessa cardui* is the scientific name of the painted lady butterfly. It is understood by Lepidopterists everywhere.

Sometimes a Lepidopterist decides that a butterfly, skipper, or moth has been improperly named. Then the scientific name may be changed. The painted lady butterfly was named *Papilio cardui* about two centuries ago by Carolus Linnaeus, the famous Swedish scientist. Many years later, it was given its present name by another scientist.

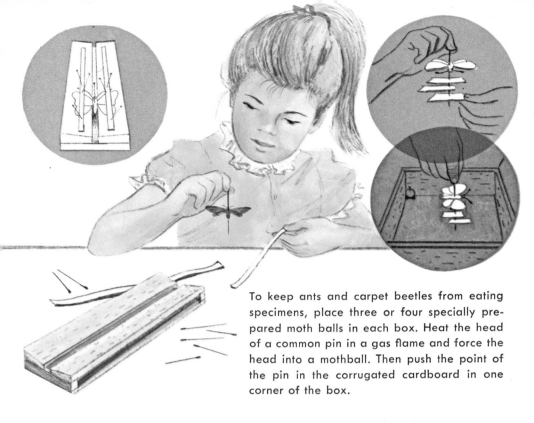

To keep ants and carpet beetles from eating specimens, place three or four specially prepared moth balls in each box. Heat the head of a common pin in a gas flame and force the head into a mothball. Then push the point of the pin in the corrugated cardboard in one corner of the box.

Storing Collections

FOR HOUSING the winged adults of a beginning Lepidoptera collection, cigar boxes will do very well. To keep the collection neat, select boxes of the same size and shape. In the bottom of each box, place a sheet or two of corrugated cardboard cut to fit.

As soon as specimens dry, they can be arranged in rows in the boxes, usually two or more kinds to a box.

48

Larvae or caterpillars can also be collected. They are killed quickly in boiling water and preserved in alcohol.

To transfer a specimen from the spreading board to a storage box, first remove the papers used to hold the wings in place. With first finger and thumb, grasp the head of the pin run through the thorax of the specimen. Lift the specimen carefully without touching it. Run the pin through the labels prepared for the specimen. Push the point of the pin straight down into the corrugated cardboard in the bottom of the box.

As the collection grows, boxes especially designed for insect collections may replace the cigar boxes. Such boxes can be bought from scientific supply companies.

Lepidoptera larvae or caterpillars, of course, cannot be kept on pins in cigar boxes. Kill them quickly by dropping them into boiling water. Allow the water to boil for one minute, then let it cool for twenty minutes. Finally drop the larvae into vials or bottles containing rubbing alcohol. In about a week, substitute fresh alcohol for old.

Lepidoptera and Damage

THE LARVAE and adults of most kinds or species of butterflies do very little damage to plants that man uses for food, clothing, shelter, or decoration. But the larvae of several species of moths are so numerous that in their feeding they do a great deal of damage. The damage is so great that some species are known by the names of the larvae; for example, European corn borer, eastern tent caterpillar, and bagworm.

On this and the following three pages are shown just a few of the Lepidoptera having larvae that do great damage.

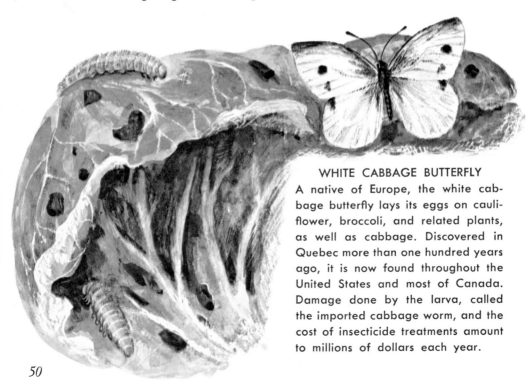

WHITE CABBAGE BUTTERFLY

A native of Europe, the white cabbage butterfly lays its eggs on cauliflower, broccoli, and related plants, as well as cabbage. Discovered in Quebec more than one hundred years ago, it is now found throughout the United States and most of Canada. Damage done by the larva, called the imported cabbage worm, and the cost of insecticide treatments amount to millions of dollars each year.

COTTON LEAFWORM
Both larva and adult of the cotton leafworm damage crops. The larva feeds on leaves of cotton plants. The adult cuts into ripe peaches with its strong, sharp beak, unusual for a moth. The insect spends the winter in Mexico and countries farther south. In spring, this moth migrates northward, sometimes in great swarms. It has as many as seven generations a year on cotton in the South.

EASTERN TENT CATERPILLAR
Apple, black cherry, box elder, and many other trees in the United States and Canada east of the Rocky Mountains may have large areas covered with unsightly brown tents or webs of the eastern tent caterpillar. Inside these tents live large numbers of caterpillars, which leave the tents during the day to feed.

INDIAN MEAL MOTH
The Indian meal moth larva eats all kinds of grain in storage, cereals, dried fruits, candy, and nuts. Commonly mistaken for the clothes moth, it is found throughout the United States. It may have as many as six generations each year. 51

CASEMAKING CLOTHES MOTH

The casemaking clothes moth, sometimes called "miller," is found throughout the world. Before man appeared on earth and built houses, the clothes moth larva ate dead insects, hair, feathers, and dead animals. In homes it feeds chiefly on woolen clothing and upholstered furniture. The tiny moth probably does not eat.

GYPSY MOTH

The gypsy moth is the most destructive leaf-feeding pest on shade and woodland trees in the northeastern part of the United States. It feeds on more than five hundred kinds of plants. Millions of dollars have been spent in fighting it. The males and females are quite different from each other in size and color.

EUROPEAN CORN BORER

The European corn borer, discovered in the United States in 1917, can live on more than two hundred kinds of plants. It is most destructive to corn. In 1949 it caused a loss estimated at 314 million bushels of corn valued at $350,000,000. It is controlled by several kinds of wasp and fly parasites, and in some areas by insecticides.

CODLING MOTH

The codling moth (the larva is the "worm in the apple") is found throughout the apple-growing sections of the world. It may destroy as much as 95 per cent of an apple crop if control measures are not used. It is usually controlled by several accurately timed applications of insecticide.

BAGWORM

The bagworm damages many kinds of trees and shrubs in the eastern half of the United States. It constructs a bag of silk to which it attaches bits of leaves from the plant on which it feeds. It lives in the bag and enlarges it as it grows. Only the male bagworm moth, rarely seen, has wings and can fly. The wingless female never leaves her bag.

TOMATO HORNWORM

The tomato hornworm, larva of a common sphinx moth, is well known as a pest to all who grow tomatoes. It is a large, smooth, green caterpillar with a spine near the end of the abdomen. In addition to tomato leaves, it eats leaves of potato, tobacco, eggplant, and pepper. It is found throughout the United States and southern Canada. Sometimes its numbers are kept low by attacks of a tiny wasp parasite.

● How Lepidoptera Are Controlled

IF ALL the moth and butterfly eggs hatched, all the larvae lived and became adults, all the adults mated, and all the females laid eggs that hatched, the Lepidoptera would soon destroy so many plants that the world would be unfit for any living thing, including themselves.

Like other insects, the Lepidoptera have many enemies that help to control them by keeping down their numbers.

Weather is one of the most powerful enemies. Beating rains, strong winds, and temperatures too hot or too cold destroy large numbers of eggs, larvae, or adults.

Birds, mammals, and reptiles are other enemies. They are called predators of the Lepidoptera because they prey upon, or eat, moth and butterfly larvae or adults.

Birds are the natural enemies of insects. They help to keep insect numbers within safe limits.

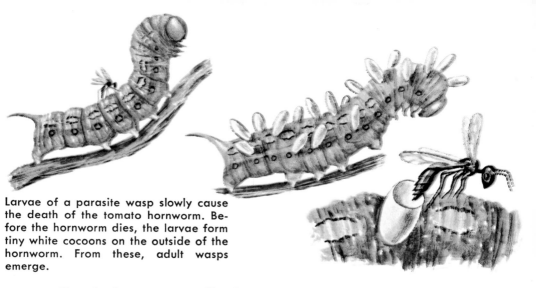

Larvae of a parasite wasp slowly cause the death of the tomato hornworm. Before the hornworm dies, the larvae form tiny white cocoons on the outside of the hornworm. From these, adult wasps emerge.

Certain insects are still other enemies of the Lepidoptera. Some are predators, preying upon or eating Lepidoptera eggs, larvae, or adults. Some are parasites. Most of these parasites are larvae of tiny wasps or flies that live within the bodies of Lepidoptera larvae or adults. For example, a tiny wasp is a parasite of the tomato hornworm. The female of this wasp lays her eggs in the hornworm. From the eggs hatch tiny larvae that feed on the inner organs of the hornworm. These larvae then form cocoons, from which adults emerge.

Diseases are still other enemies of the Lepidoptera. Weather has great influence on the diseases. A disease that is helped along by damp weather may destroy billions of moth or butterfly larvae.

Human beings also are enemies of the Lepidoptera—or at least of the kinds that damage crops. Men have tried to control the harmful Lepidoptera in two ways: first, through use of natural enemies and, second, through use of chemicals known as insecticides or insect killers.

Men have tried to protect birds, mammals, and even reptiles that prey on insects. They have discouraged the killing of insects that help to control harmful insects—for example, the lady beetle. The larva of the lady beetle feeds on the larva of the European corn borer. Men have even collected and raised natural insect enemies of some of the Lepidoptera. When the European corn borer was discovered in the United States several years ago, scientists went to the old home of the borer in Austria and collected some of its natural enemies. They brought them back to the United States and let them loose where the corn borer was doing great damage. One of these natural enemies, a hairy fly, is helping to keep down corn borer damage by destroying the larvae.

The insecticides men use to control insects are of two kinds. One kind is known as a contact poison. It kills the insect that contacts or touches it. The other kind is known as a stomach poison. It kills the insect that eats the plant that has the poison on it.

Most insecticides now used kill harmless as well as harmful insects. For this reason, efforts are being made to find insecticides that will kill only certain kinds of insects—harmful ones. Also, research is being carried on to find better ways of controlling insects through natural enemies and diseases.

Shown here are some of the many ways insects are kept under control. Larger animals or insects eat them. Severe weather destroys them. And man, using chemical sprays, kills them. Without these controls, insects would cause great damage to crops and natural plant life.

Butterflies and You

BUTTERFLIES, skippers, and moths mean different things to different persons. Just to watch a butterfly sailing on a summer breeze or feeding on a flower gives some persons pleasure. A neat collection of specimens may give some persons greater satisfaction than a stamp collection. To flower growers and farmers, certain Lepidoptera mean useful workers that carry pollen from flower to flower and help to insure good seed.

For many hundreds of years, butterflies have been studied and admired. Poets have put them in verse. Scientists have examined their form and behavior. Artists have put their colors and shapes into painting and sculpture. Musicians have set their flight to music.

In the plowing of land and in the building of cities and roads, many areas of natural beauty in the United States have been destroyed. To a person hoping to save as many as possible of the natural areas, certain butterflies are welcome signals. They show that natural areas exist nearby.

58

The Rare Ones

Schaus' Swallowtail

SOME BUTTERFLIES and moths are so un-common that collectors ought not to capture them. Most are uncommon because their habitats, the only places in which they can live, are uncommon. So both the uncommon species and the uncommon habitats should be saved.

For many years, one of the rarest butterflies in the United States was Schaus' swallowtail. It was first discovered in Miami, Florida. When growth of the city destroyed much of its habitat, it disappeared from the area. Later it was found in the Florida Keys.

In the past century, many species of North American butterflies and moths have been ex-terminated from areas where they were once abundant. Some are known by only a single specimen. If the rare ones are to be saved for future generations of Lepidopterists to enjoy, the places in which they live and the plants on which they feed must be saved.

59

WHAT IS MOON MILK?

HOW DO ENGINES WORK?

HOW DEEP CAN DIVERS GO?

Whitman
Learn About Books

THE MICROSCOPE AND A HIDDEN WORLD TO EXPLORE *Irene S. Pyszkowski*

Learn how man discovered the hidden world of the invisible. Find out how microscopes are used by detectives, scientists, doctors, and how it is possible to see tiny living things all around us.

ASTRONOMY—OUR SOLAR SYSTEM AND BEYOND *Robert I. Johnson*

Find out about the planets and moons that circle our star, the Sun. Look at actual photographs of craters on the moon, giant tornadoes on the Sun, and exploding stars millions of miles away from us.

ADVENTURES IN SCIENCE *Charles D. Neal*

Experiments to be done at home show how sound, heat, and light travel . . . why lemon juice can be used to write secret messages . . . why a can heated in just the right way crumples when it cools—and much more.

FIND OUT! FIRST STEP TO THE FUTURE *Dr. Dan Q. Posin*

Have you ever wondered how a telescope works? Or how storms happen? Or how the big electronic brains work? Or how atoms join to make all things on Earth—and in space? Dr. Posin has the answers!

ROCKETS TO EXPLORE THE UNKNOWN *Don E. Rogers*

Learn how rockets, and cannons—and bicycles!—are all a little alike. Find out how rockets work, and how they are being designed to fly faster and farther, to carry man out into unknown space.

Butterflies